P9-AFH-428

More Praise For
The Way of the Pulse: *Drumming With Spirit*

Dr. Diamond opens our eyes to the aspirational dimensions of Music and the Arts. This book reveals drumming as an activity of the Spirit, encouraging therapeutic communication through the rhythms and melodies of our souls.

RAY GRASSE, AUTHOR, *THE WAKING DREAM*

...charming, imaginative and informative!

JIM CHAPIN, MASTER DRUMMER
INTERNATIONAL RECORDING ARTIST

Dr. Diamond presents the drums as the true communicator we know them to be — I recommend this book!

BARRY GREENSPON
PRESIDENT, DRUMMER'S WORLD, INC.

All musicians aspire to move with the Pulse. This book should be read by everyone — very inspirational!

JOE PORCARO, STUDIO MUSICIAN
PROFESSIONAL DRUM INSTRUCTOR

This book represents a major step forward in our understanding of drumming as a therapeutic modality. Here is a fundamental philosophy which embraces all of music and healing.

PAUL CAVACIUTI, DIP.MUS., D.I.M.H.
FORMER HEAD OF PERCUSSION, MUSICIAN'S INSTITUTE

Dr. Diamond's book gives flight to one's imagination to go beyond the boundaries of our everyday life.

EFFIE POY YEW CHOW, PH.D., R.N., DIPL. AC.
PRESIDENT, EASTWEST ACADEMY OF HEALING ARTS

An incredible book based upon an enlightened concept — percussion for healing. Way to go, Dr. Diamond!

JOHNNY CRAVIOTTO, MASTER DRUM-MAKER

The Way
of the
Pulse

Drumming with Spirit

John Diamond, M.D.
D.P.M., F.R.A.N.Z.C.P., M.R.C. Psych.

THE WAY OF THE PULSE: Drumming with Spirit
Copyright © 1999 by John Diamond, M.D.

All rights reserved.
No portion of this book may be reproduced in any form without the permission in writing from the publisher.

Published by: Enhancement Books
                P.O. Box 544,
                Bloomingdale, IL 60108.

Printed in the United States of America
ISBN 1-890995-02-09

Cover photograph by John Diamond

Other Books by Dr. John Diamond:

Your Body Doesn't Lie
Life Energy: Unlocking the Hidden Power of Your Emotions
   to Achieve Total Well-Being
Life-Energy Analysis: A Way to Cantillation
The Re-Mothering Experience: How to Totally Love
The Life Energy in Music (The Life Energy in Music, Volume I)
The Wellspring of Music (The Life Energy in Music, Volume II)
The Heart of Music (The Life Energy in Music, Volume III)
A Spiritual Basis of Holistic Therapy
The Collected Papers, Volumes I and II
Speech, Language and the Power of the Breath
A Book of Cantillatory Poems
A Prayer On Entering: The Healer's Hearth a Sanctuary
The Healing Power of Blake: A Distillation
Life Enhancement Through Music

All books available from:
The Diamond Center
P. O. Box 381
South Salem, New York 10590 USA
(914) 533-2158

To Dear Susan, who has helped me,
through her music and her life,
to feel the Pulse.

Drumming is *Spirit. A band won't sound good
if the drummer is just beating, and has no spirit.*

*That's why all guys are not drummers that's
drumming.*

BABY DODDS
THE GREAT NEW ORLEANS DRUMMER
1898–1959

Introduction

$\mathcal{I}$ used to practice Medicine, but now – Music! The change came about as I increasingly realized that there was within us a great healing force, Life Energy. Hippocrates called this the Healing Power of Nature.

With this awareness, I became less interested in what a patient could not do, his medical diagnosis, and much more interested in what he could. This is his Creativity, and when it is energized he will choose the best path for health and life and for love.

The highest Creativity of all is Music. And it is this which I now encourage in my students – in very particular ways which I call The Way of the Pulse, which will most release the Healing Power within them.

Within music the highest forms of all are singing and dancing. So I teach my students to sing and dance on the Pulse.

And of all the instruments with which I have worked over the years, the one which is easiest to play on the Pulse, thus the one which most raises Life Energy, is the drum. So now I enthusiastically, passionately, encourage all who come to me to improve their lives to play drums.

But not to play for narcissistic, ego reasons, but from the deep desire, the aspiration, to find the Way of the Pulse, Peace and Love – and to give them to others.

Music is for giving. As Beethoven wrote, "From the heart, may it go to the heart."

This is The Way of the Pulse. This is Drumming with Spirit.

———————

Foreword

The association of drumming with spirituality is deeply rooted in the human psyche. Many cultures throughout history have been aware that the drum allows us to express more than the purely musical, to communicate on a deeper level than just the aesthetic. Where this originates, I believe, is in the fact that the drum is capable of expressing the heartbeat, the very thing that, in a sense, causes us to be. In a way, the sound of the drum is the sound of life itself.

The drum, therefore, is capable of expressing our fundamental nature. At one end of the spectrum, this means our most primitive and warlike emotions, which accounts for the drum's long-recognized cathartic potential; at the other end, it can release our highest and most essential selves. It is no accident that drumming plays an important part in many religious and Shamanic practices.

The last five years have seen an enormous growth in people's interest in the therapeutic potential of drumming. Certainly, drums have been used peripherally in a variety of therapeutic contexts for far longer, but it is only now that the idea of drumming as a therapy in itself is beginning to take off. This is best seen in the proliferation of drum circles which have achieved a great deal of popularity with people of widely differing ages and backgrounds. However, with all this burgeoning interest in the subject, it is surprising how much research still remains to be done on why drumming is such an effective healing modality.

Dr. John Diamond's *The Way of the Pulse* represents a major step forward in our understanding of this new and highly complex field. It is partly a description of techniques, partly an exploration of underlying principles, but both of these are knit together by a fundamental philosophy which embraces all of music and healing.

The concept of the Pulse is the philosophical foundation for all of Dr. Diamond's work. In many ways it is analogous to the Tao, as a metaphor for the continuum of human existence. But the word "Pulse," with its particular resonances of physiology and music, expresses much more.

There are so many different kinds of pulse – the heartbeat, the pattern of the ocean waves, the change of the seasons. These smaller pulses are reflections of The Pulse, the movement of life, which underlies everything. It is this movement and man's relation to it that philosophers and sages have attempted to describe, each in his own way, for millennia. Dr. Diamond's contribution to this has been to see that one of the ways in which we, as individuals, can feel this movement is through music, and most effectively through the drum.

In this sense, the Pulse also provides the conceptual basis for the relationship between music and healing. As many healers have taught since the time of Pythagoras, when we move with the flow of life, we reduce stress and help our minds and bodies function as they are intended to. When we go aginst that flow, life becomes difficult and we suffer, first emotionally and later physically. Learning to feel The Pulse in music can help us to actually experience that flow in ourselves and in others. Once we begin to feel it, we *know* whether we are moving with it or not and can make decisions accordingly.

This awareness can help us, among other things, in our ability to integrate and overcome emotional trauma, to improve our neurological processing and to release physical tension. Ultimately, to flow with The Pulse activates our own natural desire for health, which is the most important step to achieving it.

As Lao Tzu wrote: "The Way that can be spoken of is not the true Way." Certainly, many people have read books about the Tao, but how many can really say that they live their lives in harmony with it? Understanding the Pulse as an idea is not enough, we need to actually feel it, and this is where *Drumming with Spirit* comes in.

The approach to drumming that this book documents is unique in several ways, but perhaps the area in which it differs most from other methodologies is in its exploration of the specific process involved in making drumming therapeutic. It is worth remembering that the writer came to his practical and philosophical conclusions first as a healer and then as a drummer.

Dr. Diamond was fully qualified in medicine, psychiatry and preventive medicine, with thirty years of clinical experience, before he ever held a pair of sticks in his hands. This has given him a perspective uncluttered by any professional, technical, artistic or traditional preconceptions, and has allowed him to focus solely on how to make drumming a truly therapeutic activity. Speaking as a professional drummer, I cannot emphasize enough what a difference this makes!

Furthermore, his experience in so many different areas of conventional and complementary medicine has given him tools to develop objective clinical criteria to evaluate the actual therapeutic benefits derived from a particular approach. In many ways, this fact alone sets his work apart from anyone else's in this field.

In Dr. Diamond's approach, the therapy does not reside so much with the drums themselves, as in their ability to help us feel the Pulse in music. The drums have several advantages over other instruments in this regard.

The main advantage is that we can play a song without worrying about playing "wrong" notes. This removes one of the main inhibitions that people experience playing music. Also, using a drum *set* allows us to involve our *entire* body: by bringing the feet into the act of music-making, we incorporate the body's natural tendency to move in response to music.

These factors help us to make music in a way that is stress-free, both physiologically and psychologically, and that allows us to focus on the *movement* of the music rather than the notes or the technique. In this way the drumming becomes a living metaphor for the Pulse itself. As we begin to experience that ease and flow in the drumming, it becomes possible for us to take that feeling into other areas of our lives: our work, our relationships, and our attitudes towards ourselves. Only then can we really begin to actuate the forces of self-healing that exist within us all.

With *The Way of the Pulse*, Dr. Diamond has arrived at a highly sophisticated and original way of looking at music and its relationship to health. But more than that, he has given us a genuinely new way of looking at spiritual and philosophical ideas which have been around for thousands of years, and has shown us how we can integrate them into our everyday existence.

This is not just a book for drummers, or even therapists: this is a book for everyone who is interested in living a more expansive, creative and stress-free life.

PAUL CAVACIUTI, DIP.MUS., D.I.M.H.
INTERNATIONAL RECORDING ARTIST
FORMER HEAD OF PERCUSSION, MUSICIAN'S INSTITUTE

Life
is Ol' Man River.
We can roll along
with it,
or try, vainly,
to swim against.

Start by singing it,
drumming it,
as it goes
– as it rolls.
And your life
will follow along.

The Way of the Pulse is about how to live our lives with joy and love – using drumming as a metaphor. For as in music, so in life.

And it is for the musician, from beginner to professional, to help him realize that there is this other way. That life – and music – can come from the soul.

This book is for all who know in their heart that there is more to music and life than just playing and living on the beat. For those who wish to live and play the other way, The Way of the Pulse – one with Spirit. For all who want to love through music, to live as Music.

And it is for all who have yearned to play the drums – and that is everyone! To play for enjoyment, and more – to play for Life and Love – with Spirit! This is the way to begin.

————————

From the heart
of the Muse,
the waves of Her pulse
flow through us
as Spirit.

The concept of the Pulse is the summation and the culmination of all my years in medicine, in psychiatry, in complementary medicine, in holistic healing – and in music.

And it is my hope that this may help you to suffer a little less in life – and to be able to embrace it joyfully, enthusiastically, and gratefully.

Regardless of their particular words, their metaphors, and their techniques, this seems to be the central teaching of all the healing modalities.

———

I look
at my hands moving.
They are my hands,
but not me moving.
They are being moved
by the Pulse,
the way of the song.

The Tide and The Pulse

"There is a tide in the affairs of men," Shakespeare proclaimed. Not a force or power, or a direction, but a tide.

A tide: ebb and flow, ebb and flow. Movement, always movement; ever changing yet ever recurring. And always advancing through time – to where? To where? Back and forth, round and round, and on and on.

I stand on a cliff overlooking the beach I have loved all my life and I realize it is not the sand or the water that draws me, but the waves, the exquisite dancing creations of tide and wind, of earth's turning, of the dance of sun with moon.

I watch as each of them washes over the rock beneath me, each forming its own pattern of movement, of white, of life. Each forward and back, and around and around – and then on to the next, and the next, and the next.

And I start to move with the waves, to dance with them as they flow over the rock, covering it, revealing it and covering it again. Each with its own delightful dance. "When you do dance, I wish you a wave o' the sea." Shakespeare knew. Oh yes, he knew.

Of course God is a singer – every Mother is. But if he also plays an instrument, then he is certainly a percussionist, not a violinist, or, God forbid, a pianist! For it is not the notes He cares about, not the much vaunted harmony, but the basic rhythm, the propelling power, the Pulse itself. And it is to this that I dance with the waves. "When you do dance, I wish you a wave o' the sea." Shakespeare knew. Oh yes.

I do not know what Tao meant to the ancient Chinese, but certainly its translation into The Way is quite inadequate. Colorless, bland, lifeless somehow. There is a sense of direction, yes, but not of movement, of propulsion, of power. All this the word Pulse possesses and so much more: the Pulse is love. It is the sound we hear inside the Mother's womb, back and forth, back and forth. And when She cradles us in Her arms and rocks us back and forth, it is to the Pulse, always to the Pulse.

This is the "tide in the affairs of men." And it is this Love that impels the tide as it always has, and as it always will: the pulsation back and forth, from her heart to ours, and from ours to Hers: back and forth, around and around.

The Heart
of Love
impels
the Pulse.

———

Drumming, Pulse & Tao

*I*t is said that "all things emerge from the Tao in creation as babies emerge from their mothers . . . But the Way does not simply give birth to all things. Having done so, it continues in some way to be present in each individual thing as an energy or power, a power that is not static but constantly on the move, inwardly pushing each thing to develop and grow in a certain way in a way that is in accord with its true nature."[1]

And the particular way which the thing, a person, a song, moves is its Pulse.

And I believe that if we could, as it were, swim up the stream of a particular pulse, getting closer and closer to its source, to its fountainhead, we would then find that all the apparently infinite pulse forms are really one and the same.

Then in this state of the highest enlightenment, we would finally understand the Way – we would at last know the ultimate reality.

---

[1] Lao-Tzu, *Te-Tao Ching*, transl. Robert G. Hendricks. Ballantine Books. 1989.

So we start with drumming, not knowing how far we will go. But allowing the Way, submitting to the Pulse.

———————

The Drum and The Mother

The basic problem of all existence, the root cause of all human suffering, is alienation from the mother. She was the whole world to us – the source of all love, and the cause of all distress. Reconciliation with her, the grateful reunion, is the task of life. This is the way, the only way, to love and enlightenment. Our homage to maternal love.

And of everything on earth, music can most remind us of her love, and her intention to love, for it came from her, her at her purest, her most Perfect. The pulsations of her body, her rocking, her lilt and her lullaby.

The drum takes us back to the womb, to the world of rhythm. Her rhythm – the pulsation of her heart. So, of all instruments, the drum is the most basic, the most archaic, and (potentially) the most loving.

Her heartbeat
the first Muse message.
Drumming,
the belated reply.

"Creation arises from the drum," proclaims an ancient Hindu text.

And the drum is played by Shiva, the Highest God, the God of the Universe. And Shiva is the Lord of Dance. He drums and dances, and all the Universe dances to Him.

His dance, and thus ours, is "His mystery play of continuous creation."

His drumming, His dance. This is what I mean by the Way of the Pulse.

And Shiva is usually depicted dancing, holding a drum and making the sign of "Do not fear."

Just surrender to His drumming, to the Way. Do not fear. Accept It, embrace It. Wholeheartedly, gratefully. Drum with It so as to move with It so as to be One with It.

This is what I mean by Drumming with Spirit.

———

When you are playing on the Pulse,
it feels like the drum
is playing you.

The pulse of the flowing sea.

MORICE

*P*ity the poor swimmer who, ignoring the wave, must beat his way to the shore. But the one who catches it will have an easy, effortless ride.

And best is to ride not on the crest of the wave, for then you can fall off it, but instead to be just a little ahead of it – like when surfing.

> Play on the pulse
> and the wave brings you
> to the shore,
> effortlessly.

———

The drummer
is a sculptor,
fashioning in sound
the particular pulse forms
of each piece.

Playing on the pulse
is making waves
on water.

The Pulse

My soul is an enchanted boat,
Which, like a sleeping swan, doth float
Upon the silver waves of thy sweet singing.

SHELLEY

The pulse, the mother, music and water. Let's see now if we can draw all this together.

When we think of the word *pulse*, words invoking fluidity come to us like *blood, flow,* and *waves.* One of the Oxford English Dictionary (OED) definitions of *pulse* is "the rhythmical recurrence of . . . undulations."

It gives this illustrative quotation: "like the pulse of the flowing sea." And the American Heritage Dictionary (AHD) definition of *pulsate* is "to expand and contract rhythmically." It goes on: "recurrent rhythmical movements like those involved in the periodic expansion and contraction of the heart." So we have undulations, flow, sea, rhythm, and heart.

And what of *undulate*? "To cause to move in a smooth wavelike motion" (AHD). It is derived from the Indo-European root *wed* – water, wet. From which have arisen such words as *water, wet, wash, winter, hydro, dropsy, undulate, redundant, whisky,* and *vodka.*

And what of *wave*? "A movement in the sea or other collection of water, by which a portion of the water rises above the normal level and then subsides, at the same time travelling a greater or smaller distance over the surface; a moving . . . swell of water.[2]

Now let's examine a number of words, all starting with *fl. Fluid* : "flowing or moving readily."

Flux: "the flowing of the tide." "The sea undergoes a flux and reflux." Another definition: "a continuous succession of changes of condition." And this wonderful quote from Butler (1736): "the bodies of all animals are in a constant flux."

And *fluctuate*: "To rise and fall in or as in waves." "To undulate." And again the allusion to water in this quotation from Pecke (1659): "I can't call him Rich, or Poor; whose estates upon deluding waters, fluctuate."

So *pulse* and *undulate* and *wave* and *fluid* and *flux* all basically have to do with movement and water, and its ever-changing nature.

Let us turn now to that most wonderous collection of knowledge, *The Origins of European Thought* by R. B. Onians.[3] I will give just a few points, briefly stated.

---

[2] All following definitions are from The Oxford English Dictionary.
[3] Cambridge University Press. 1951

In ancient times, the Muses were water nymphs, and poets drank of their springs. A poem was water, honey or nectar of the Muses. And Pindar wrote that water is the best of all things. Water was the life-substance. In the Koran we read that God created every beast from water.

And now this quote from Onians: "That water is life is nowhere more strikingly illustrated than the actual experience of frogs in Mediterranean and similar climes. There is a hymn in the Rig Veda about their reawakening after the dry season: When the waters from the sky fall upon them as they lie like a dried skin in the (dried up) pond, the voice of the frogs rises in concert."[4]

So, the Water of Life. Life is liquid. Hence there was river-worship. "God of liquid, the life-giving stream."[5]

The head of the body was the source, the fountainhead of liquid. "The brain with its fluid was the stuff . . . of generation."[6]

So we have all these threads:

Water is the life-substance. Running water, river-worship. Running water in flux. Pulsations, waves, and undulations. The head, the fountainhead. The Muses as water nymphs (and the word muse comes from the Indo-European root *men* – to think). And a poem (and a song) is water. And the mother is water, and blood, and milk.

---

[4] p. 291.
[5] p. 229.
[6] p. 227.

Source, flow, wave, and pulsation. Water and Muse, water and mother. Water and song, and song comes from the mother.

Each song springs from the Muse's watery fountainhead. Imbued with the Life Element it flows down the river of life, propelled along in a series of utterly unique, undulating, fluctuating waves which are the particular pulse forms for each phrase of that song, and for every moment of our lives.

"The Mother is water. The Great Goddess is the flowing unity of subterranean and celestial primordial water, the sea of heaven ... the circular life-generating ocean above and below the earth. To her belong all waters, streams, fountains, ponds and springs, as well as the rain. She is the ocean of life with its life-and-death-bringing seasons, and life is her child."[7] And the Great Goddess, The Mother, is the Perfection which is everyone's mother.

Not only is music associated with The Mother, with our mothers – but especially so is the drum.

Marija Gimbutas, drawing on her most extensive analysis of the signs and design patterns that appear repeatedly in the cult objects and painted pottery of Neolithic Europe, writes concerning the Goddess and music about "the intimate relation between the drum and the Goddess." That "the most explicit decoration consists of breasts, a pair on either side of the (clay) drum ... Further evidence for this relation between the drum and the Goddess comes

---

[7] Erich Neumann, *The Great Mother*. Princeton University Press. 1963. p. 222.

from the Bronze Age ... three chalk drums were recovered from a child's grave ... the main panel in the center of two of the drums is dominated by the face of the Goddess."[8]

The Goddess who is our mother, is the water (the amniotic fluid, the milk, the water of life), the vessel that contains (the womb, her body, her breasts), and she is the drum, the vessel that gives us the undulations, the waves of water, the essence of music, the rhythm – Her rhythm.

So the drum is your Mother. Treat her accordingly.

———————

———————

[8] *The Language of the Goddess*. Harper and Row, San Francisco. 1989. p.71.

Imagine the drum
is your mother.
Don't hit her —
just nudge her
to sing.

Beat Versus Pulse

*A*ll music comes from the mother. From the rhythmic pulsation which we felt when inside her, and then later from her cradling and rocking, her lilt and her lullaby. And all love came from her – and all negativity. Within each of us there are two mothers, the one we know who loves us – and the one we fear, the one we must obey: "She who must be obeyed."

When we feel loved by her, we move through life effortlessly, gracefully, as if we were still in her arms rocked by the movement of her body, reassured by her smile, comforted by her song. This is living life on the pulse, the rhythmic gentle undulation of the mother, of life itself. This is peace, this is tranquility. This is love.

But life on the beat is the very opposite. It is imposed on us. It is the feared schoolteacher tapping his cane, warningly, menacingly. It is so often, unfortunately, the conductor's baton: not the open hands of the loving mother, but the sceptre of domination. Not a life of love, but one of fear. Not our free choice to act from the highest intention but servile submission, fearful obedience. Not freedom, but usury.

And as in life, so in music. We can play on the pulse, truly, effortlessly, lovingly. Or on the beat – the metronome being the mother who must be obeyed. And it is not play, for there is no enjoyment – it is work, and hard work, for there is no love.

We have a choice to be coldly accurate, like a machine, or to be human. To submit to the domination of the beat, or to flow with the Pulse of love and life.

We just need to find Her, move with Her, play with Her – the Mother of Love. Then we become True Musicians – true to the real purpose of Music, validating Its, and our, Existence.

———

Each drum
a resonant heart.
Tap it –
feel its pulse.

No two waves
are ever the same,
not in the ocean,
nor in our bodies.
The heart, thank God,
is not a metronome.

I am real, I'm alive.
I breathe.
I pulsate.
I am not a machine.
If they want the beat –
they can buy a metronome.

$\mathcal{T}$oscanini was once congratulated after a performance of Beethoven's Ninth Symphony by a member of the audience who told him that he had previously heard him conduct the same work some thirty years previously. And, he went on to say, the performance was identical. Toscanini told him this was not the case – his pulse rate had been different on that occasion.

Not the tempi, not the metronome beats, but his pulse rate: the undulating surge of life through his body. I understand that before the invention of the metronome, it was common practice to relate the tempo of the piece to the pulse rate of the performer.

And the pulse rate is constantly changing, for it is not mechanical but alive, and a fundamental property of living matter is that it is ever changing, never regular. So it is, too, with music, for music is alive, so alive.

No two lines of poetry, even with the same number of syllables, are of equal length over time. No two syllables quite the same, nor any two heartbeats. So to recite a poem, to sing a song, or to drum to it, we need to be constantly adjusting to the time length of every word, of every syllable, and every phrase, and to the differing movements between any two of them.

And the more we understand the song, the deeper we go into it, the closer we will come to its true inner nature, its inner pulsation, which is what I call its Pulse.

There is a center inside our brains which determines the pulsation of the heart from moment to moment, and there is, as it were, a center inside the composer which determines the pulse rate of his song from moment to moment, from note to note.

It is my conviction that the true purpose of every musician is to bring forth, to manifest, this inner deeper pulsation, the Pulse of each song. The drummer's role in this is crucial, for he, most of all, can delineate the pulse for his fellow musicians as well as for the audience. But if instead, he ignores this and concentrates on a fixed, regular, unnatural beat, then he will be not the living heart of the band, but only its pacemaker.

Gershwin was not a machine but a human being. Help them to feel his heartbeat, his breathing and, underlying them, his Pulse.

———

Our breathing changes
with every thought,
with every feeling,
with every movement,
and likewise
our heart rate.
This is the way
of Nature.

And so too,
the pulse of the music
is in constant flux
as it shapes
every note, every phrase.
For music, too,
True Music,
comes from our deepest
Nature.

The beat
bars the way
to the Muse.
The pulse
propels you
to Her.

Life pulsates.

EMERSON

$\mathcal{A}$ pulse rate of sixty per minute is not one per second, but sixty measured over a minute. It is not metronomically precise. It is not a click track.

The pulse is constantly changing, being affected by any and every alteration in the individual's physiology and psychology.

Feel it change now with your breathing, with your thoughts. It is alive. It is Nature. The pulse is the waveform that transports the life blood throughout the body. And the pulse of the music is the rhythmically recurrent undulations that are the life force that propels the music, emanating from its very heart.

Metronome – beat;
heart – pulse.

—————

Beats are sudden, sharp.
Isolated.
Down.
Hurtful. Dictatorial.

The Pulse is continuous,
ever flowing.
Gentle, uplifting.
It comforts. It supports.
The Pulse is Love.

Beat: the hit,
pulse: the heart.

The beat:
She who
must
be obeyed!

The pulse:
how the music goes.
The beat:
how I will
make it go.

Get on the wave of the Pulse,
and ride it effortlessly
all the way to the beach.
With the beat,
you must paddle like mad.

Beat
or pulse –
your way,
or Hers.

The beat is fear
of the mother,
the pulse –
loving reunion.

The beat:
life to a
click track.

To Beat or to Actuate

*F*rom my psychiatric training I have learned to listen very carefully to the words we use. To examine them for deeper underlying meanings. The parent who calls his child "the little devil," however much he smiles when saying it, is often telling me a great deal about his inner attitude, his truer feelings.

With this in mind, consider the words we almost invariably use to describe the act of bringing the hand or stick into contact with the drumhead: *hit, beat,* or *strike.* Herein lies one of the major problems with drumming, for no instrument is so abused, and none deserves it less. For the drum can be the most Life Energy enhancing, the most healing instrument of them all. This is inherent in its basic design. It just requires the correct attitude, the right intention, to release this most wonderful innate power.

Let's look at some of the definitions of these words.

Firstly, *hit*: to strike or deal a blow to. To strike with a missile. To affect adversely.

And here are some of the synonyms for *hit*: strike, cuff, knock, bash, thump, punch, buffet, slap, swat, spank, beat, batter, belabor, clout, smite, thwack, wack, sock, bludgeon, club, clobber, thrash, pummel, flog, scourge, cane, lash, flagellate, whip.

Hardly healing!

And what of *beat*? To strike repeatedly. To punish by hitting or whipping; flog. To strike against repeatedly and with force; pound. To shape or break by repeated blows. To defeat or subdue. To inflict repeated blows.

The central meaning being to hit heavily and repeatedly with violent blows. Can you imagine using a word like this with the violin?

And *strike*: To hit sharply, as with the hand, a fist, or a weapon. To inflict (a blow). To collide with or crash into. To cause to come into violent or forceful contact. To damage or destroy, as by forceful contact. To make a military attack on; assault. To afflict suddenly, as with a disease or impairment.

If these are the verbs we use to describe each and every act of producing music from a drum, then there must be something wrong, or potentially wrong, with our basic attitude. For to use the word is to invoke its feeling. And furthermore, this negativity is transmitted in the music.

Conversely, if we can find a better word, perhaps it will help to change our underlying attitude, enabling us to help the drum release its therapeutic potential, its power for love. For no instrument can do this better – when played with the right basic attitude.

Let us now instead consider the word *activate*: To make active, bring into action. Cause reaction in; excite.

This would certainly be a better word, much better. Rather than using one which invokes (albeit unconsciously) the sadistic inflicting of blows on the instrument, we think instead of activating it – bringing it to life.

And there is a word which is even better – *actuate*: To cause the operation of. To communicate motion to. It is similar to *activate* but there is an essential difference which we will now examine.

The Oxford English Dictionary gives this quotation for *activate*: "Snow and Ice . . . their cold activated by nitre or salt, will turn water into ice." The nitre or salt, as it were, puts the energy into the snow and ice. And for *actuate*: "A vibrating diaphragm could be actuated by the human voice."

To activate is to put energy into, whereas to actuate is to bring into motion the energy already present in latent form. We only change what is already there. That is to say, with actuation we just transmute the nature of the energy from potential to kinetic. We merely cause the stored-up energy to be released. You need only actuate a device or an instrument that is primed, programmed, ready to go. You are only required to press its button.

Musical instruments require only actuation, and the better they are, the more enthusiastically they respond.

To get a musical sound from a block of wood you first have to activate it, but then from a woodblock you need only to actuate it. The maker has already tranformed it from being just a block of wood, he has already activated it. All we do is release the energy he has put in. And the better the maker, the more activation, the more potential for actuation he has imparted to it. With the woodblock, I don't, as it were, make the sound, I only make it audible.

You need to *activate* a practice pad, but need only to *actuate* a drum. And never to hit or beat it!

The drum has high Life Energy, very high. It is expectantly active. Feel it as you speak, as you sing. It responds – it moves! It is quivering with expectancy. Ever alert, eagerly awaiting, imploring your touch – your actuation.

In my heart I believe that the drum is always making music, my actions merely making its innate Music manifest.

Every musical instrument has a soul, and the drum the biggest and the most responsive of all. However, if you beat it, the soul cringes in fear. But if you actuate it, if you sense its innate Being and reverence it accordingly, you can help Music to fulfill its promise as a most wondrous Healing Power.

> You don't
> make the sound,
> you just
> release it.

––––––––––

The salesman
strikes the drum
hard, again and again.

You wouldn't
buy a dog
that had been beaten
like that.

Attended
a drum concert
last night –
three hours of
beating anger.
Today my muse
is battered,
abused –
– but She'll recover.

That beautiful drum!
How can you
hit it like that!
Please don't
beat it
any more.

The drum,
she sings
while I play.

Sometimes
she continues
long after.

Seated on his throne,
the drummer must make
a kingly choice.
Will he subject the music
to his sceptral beat,
or himself submit
to the higher Power, the Pulse?

From its beat-imposed prison,
music cries out to be free.
Where is its Tom Paine?
Who will proclaim
the Rights of Music?

Tempo and Time, Or the Pulse

$\mathcal{T}$he True Drummer plays the pulse, but how to do this when he is expected to play the beat, its very antithesis?

The tempo and the time are two components of the beat. Let's first consider tempo, the speed of the music. For strict dance music and marching this should be constant, unchanging from the beginning to the end of the piece. But should this be so for other music? In classical music it changes frequently, in keeping with the changing mood of the music. And so too with popular song, the verse and the chorus are very frequently at different tempi, and often as well the A and B sections of the chorus. Again, changing in accord with the changing moods of the music.

And there is no reason why the tempo in jazz music should also not change as the emotions of the players change. It is their feelings that should determine the tempo, not the inflexible, rigid, unfeeling beat imposed by the drummer. They should be free to let their changing emotions set the tempi, rather than submitting to the unchanging, remorseless beat. Let the drummer, too, be free with his tempi – adding his contribution to the shared summated emotion of the group. He is not needed for strict tempo, for there should not be any.

The time of the music is its meter – 3/4, 4/4, etc. And no competent musician requires this to be imposed on him. It is so natural and so basic and was taught to them many years ago, at the very beginning of their musical training.

The drummer is not needed for the tempo or for the time. So what then is his function? Now that he has been liberated from the beat, he is free to endeavor to play the melody, and through this to shape and form and then display the pulse of the music to his fellow musicians.

The drummer should not be needed to control the group but rather to encourage its members to be free, free to feel the pulse and move with it. Through this group process, instigated by the drummer, they may all become True Musicians.

———

The drummer,
unlike all of his colleagues,
is free from the fear
of playing a wrong note.
But instead he suffers
to keep "perfect time."
Music is cursed
by these tyrannies.

Music has so many
musts,
all imposed by those
who deny its Spirit.

At kindergarten,
the child is taught
to count, exactly,
boringly, by rote:
1-2-3, 1-2-3.

As he grows up,
this becomes
ever more subtle:
from arithmetic
to math.

But not so for
the poor drummer.
He, they command,
must stay at the childish
1-2-3, 1-2-3.

Then they say
he's not mature!

The DD Blues

*B*ack in the old days when I first practiced medicine, it was the custom to state the occupation of most wives as "DD," short for "domestic duties." The husband may have been a director, but she was just a DD. And furthermore, frequently she would describe sexual intercourse with him as her "wifely duties." "I didn't want to do it, Doctor, but I had to give it to him. It was one of my duties."

That sums up what the word *duties* means to us.

I was reminded of this when I read the statement of one great drummer, Cliff Leeman, about another, Ray McKinley: "He never ignored his timekeeping duties."

Occupation? DD – drumming duties. A tragic reality of the usual state of drumming today. But to overcome this you just need to drum with spirit and on the pulse!

———————

Are you trying
to keep "perfect time,"
or are you aspiring
to be Perfect
in time?
That's the True Musician.

Time can't be perfect,
only our use of it.

My grandmother, a wonderful cook, never weighed or counted the ingredients for her recipes. "How much sugar do you put in, Nanna?" "Some," she'd smile. In her heart she always knew just how much.

And her pies were always perfect.

And that is how music should be – from the heart, not the brain. Just like Grandma's cooking.

———————

Play
from your muse,
not your brain.

Don't count – feel.
When the math comes in,
the joy goes out.

Music slain
by the arrows
of numbers.

Never practice
– that's just the brain.
Even if the audience is afar,
always play to them.
That's the heart as well.

Math is not music.
Math is brain.
Music, True Music,
is the heart.

Play with all your heart:
wholehearted.
And with Passion:
all your fire.
And filled
with Enthusiasm!

Painting by numbers
is not art,
sex by numbers
is not love,
and playing by numbers
is not True Music.

If you want to know
the rhythm of a song,
walk with it, dance to it.
Then transfer that
to your feet and hands.

Rhythm and Bondage

"*R*ooted deep in physiological grounds as the function of our bodies, rhythm permeates melody, form, and harmony; it becomes the driving and shaping force, indeed, the very breath of music, and reaches up into the loftiest realm of aesthetic experience where description is doomed to fail because no language provides the vocabulary for adequate wording."[1]

And it is the drummer that initiates and impels the rhythm that actuates the other musicians, and through them the audience. And the more he plays on the pulse, the loftier will be the experience.

Around 400 AD, Charisius declared: "metre is bonded rhythm." Release the rhythm, liberate the music. Play on the pulse.

---

[1] Curt Sachs, *Rhythm and Tempo*. Norton, NY. 1953.

The withered, twisted,
blind old man
seems unconscious –
till you notice
his outstretched finger
tapping out the rhythm
of our song
on the very edge
of the drum.

Like he's reaching for life.

A Rhythm, Melody or Pulse Instrument?

The didjeridu, and the drum, are labelled rhythm instruments. More than labelled, they are stigmatized – the so-called melody instruments are said to be more "musical." And likewise the didjeridu player, and the drummer, are thought to be lesser musicians.

And yet the very name didjeridu comes from a common vocalization pattern that was played, rather sung, through it. I spent many years trying to learn the pulse of songs by singing them through the didjeridu. What came out was not the words, but it certainly was not the beat. It was something approaching the pulse.

Quite often, a listener could identify the song from its pulse form (and if not, he certainly could after it was pointed out to him). It is much more identifiable than just the rhythm, yet a little less so than the melody. This is the pulse of the song.

And each vocalization pattern was unique for each song, as is its pulse form. For the pulse is the deep Muse-originating waveform unique not only for each song, but for each phrase of the song.

So the didjeridu is more than "just" a rhythm instrument And it is more than "only" a melody instrument.

Through it we can play the pulse, and it is the pulse that transports us to the Muse, to the Perfection within the song, and within the composer, and our mothers and all others around us, and ourselves.

And, if we so choose, the drum too can become a pulse instrument.

The drum as pulsator,
the drummer its actuator.

———————

There is no clear distinction
between melody and rhythm.
There is rhythm in every melody,
and melody in every rhythm.
So, let your drumming sing
– play the melody.

The drummer
doesn't play the tune.
Instead,
he imposes on it
predetermined
pieces of patterns.

But they never
quite fit,
like forcing
a jigsaw puzzle.

No other musician
deludes himself
that the work
is composed of bits
of exercise scales
that just need to be
strung together.

"A String of Pearls"
is not
a string of paradiddles.

Paradiddle, paradiddle,
fol-lol-lay!

Rhythm is melody deprived of its pitch.

SCHOPENHAUER

There's just as much music in a drum as there is in a piano, trumpet or any other instrument and I believe it can be gotten out . . . to bring melody out of drums. It may not be a melody in a certain key, like a trumpet melody, but when the snare drum picks it up, you'll know it's the same tune the trumpet or the band has just got through playing . . . .

My intention has always been to bring melody out of drums. I think it can be done and I think I shall do it one day.

BABY DODDS

And through the melody impelled by the rhythm, the drummer will come to find the pulse. And of all musicians, he will find it first, being endowed with the strongest rhythm, and now with melody as well.

———

Drum solo?
Yes – if it's
playing the melody.

If music is melody and rhythm,
and rhythm is melody without pitch,
then music is really rhythm
with some superadded pitch.
So it's the drummer who has
most of the music –
the moreso when he is playing
the melody as well.

Neither rhythm nor melody
matter in themselves.
They are each just ways to the Pulse.
Both together
make it easier:
rhythmatize the words,
vocalise the rhythm.
Sing and drum
– drum and sing.

By "sing,"
I don't mean
only melody,
but every thought,
every movement,
every beat and breath –
the totality
of your every moment,
the music of your life.

Drumming
is shaping
and lifting
the pulse forms,
the waves,
of each song.

There are many activities to do before you start to drum.

The first of these is singing. Sing the song over and over until you really know how it goes; until you feel its movement; until you begin with your hands to shape the wave-like form of its pulse.

Be very aware of your breathing – this is one of the great advantages of singing the song when you are drumming it. Drummers can ignore their breathing, but not a singer. Become aware of the end of each phrase and the need for a new breath. But do not breathe – instead just wait, and allow the breath to come in. Don't say to yourself "I am breathing" – but much better, "I am being breathed" – breathed by the muse of the song. Be passive in this process.

Often in my teaching I now introduce the poi. The poi is a ball on the end of a string which the Maoris twirl in the most incredibly beautiful patterns. I have students sing as they swing the poi in front of them in a figure eight pattern. It is almost impossible to sing on the beat when the poi is flying so easily, so beautifully, before you. You just sing to it and you are immediately on the pulse, deep into the song, feeling its love, and giving it back to the poi and out into the world. There is something miraculous about the poi, something almost supernatural; it Knows.

Now you are starting to go deeper into the song, and this will greatly enhance your drumming.

But before you take up your drum, start by accenting the pulse form that you have delineated with the free waving movements of your hands. Each hand should float like a feather or like a bird flying out away from you and then returning to fly away again with each new phrase. Don't conduct on the beat but allow your hands and arms to be carried effortlessly through the air.

Now tap your feet in synchrony with the pulse form, not a steady beat but the pulse. Go with the heart of the song, with its muse.

Now you are ready to use the hands in the manner of drumming. First you may just like to click your fingers to the pulse (best is thumb and middle finger) or you may like to start by just tapping your hands on your thighs.

And now you come to use your own drum – your very own – your belly. Tap your hands on your belly and feel the resonance throughout your body, and now tap on your chest, the habitation of your heart.

There is also a particular problem with nearly all drums when played with the hands, and that is we don't usually play them with all of the hand; the thumbs are virtually never involved. And yet the ability to use the thumb so freely is one of the unique characteristics of us as humans. Try as best you can to involve these wonderful evolutionary gifts, your thumbs, in your drumming. You will feel the difference in the Life Energy when you can do so.

Tap out the pulse with just one finger of each hand. Listen how each finger makes a slightly different sound, how each one energizes you in a different way and to a differing degree.

The question we need to ask with the drum is, "do we use the hands or drumsticks?" I have found that, all other factors being equal, the Life Energy is always much more greatly enhanced when drumsticks are used rather than the hands. I believe that the reason for this may well be that with sticks we can play more precisely on the pulse.

But before you use the drumsticks, try this first: take two hollow rods, for example of paper, or thin plastic and pat them on your belly or on the table. That too is life-enhancing music. You can make it everywhere and anywhere with these tubes of paper, with your fingers, with your hands, with your feet, with your belly, and *always* with your voice.

When holding the drumsticks, have your palms upward with the sticks resting in them. Later you may decide to change to a more conventional grip, but start this way because it opens your breathing, and, most significantly, is a gesture of giving.

Now your feet and your hands are playing, and you are singing. Go through your body and involve every muscle. Let your whole body make the music. Feel it flowing through you – and out from you.

Sing and drum from your heart. Let your whole body sing and play – let it all be at the service of your heart.

Now, pick up your drum and sing into it. Feel it vibrate in sympathy and feel the Life Energy already in it. It is not just wood; it is a drum. It has been activated, energized, by its maker. All you do now is to actuate and release that energy imparted by its creator. The drum is the most sympathetic of all instruments; sing into it; feel its immediate loving response.

Now you are ready to drum!

———————

Go into
your instrument,
right in.
Feel it's
Thusness,
unique.
Then help
to release it
into the world.

Give all of yourself.
Here I am!
This is *me*!
All of me – *now*!

You can transmit
your spirit
through your drumming.
Or, better,
by your playing
you can invoke
the spirit
within the drum.

Or, even better,
you can first
feel the spirit
that is the drum,
and allow it
to play you.

She's eighty five,
feeble, virtually blind.
"I used to play the piano,
but not for many years now.
Too old, too old.
Don't push me! I won't."
She wants to die.

What would you like to do?
She lights up:
"Just once – the drums."

For an hour or more
she plays them –
exquisite, delicate,
open hearted,
deep into the pulse
of each song.

Tune after tune,
with each one
growing younger.

And she smiles
and smiles,
filled with love
for life.

Play with joy,
with a smile.
If you're not enjoying it
– stop.

Always keep in mind
that all of you,
your Totality –
body, mind, and spirit –
is transmitted
in each and every note.

*E*ven if you are using a hand drum, it is essential that you play with your feet as well. In fact, foot drumming is even more important than hand drumming. It is in our physiology to move our feet when we move our hands, and even more so with music. So if you drum with both feet, this will help balance both the right and left hemispheres of the brain which will then help your music to be more healing.

Do not play the beat with the feet, but instead the pulse, the "bass line lullaby." This "bass line lullaby" is present in all music, but it is first most easily heard in the left hand of a loving pianist. It is a seemingly continuous rolling movement, like circular rocking.

Try this movement with your feet – don't tap out the beat, but rather express this deeper underlying pulse. It is not so much in the note but in the rolling movement *between* the notes.

So always start with the feet and concentrate more on them, for the bass is basic and the bass drum will provide the foundation, the "bass line lullaby" on top of which you can now play the melody with your hands.

Hear the lullaby
in the bass.
Feel it.
Let it roll
around and
around.

I have found after research with many groups, that the larger the group the more problems there will be. Usually, any number of players over three can cause confusion and inner chaos, which can greatly debase rather than enhance the Life Energy. And this means that the group ends up playing on the beat instead of the Pulse.

One way to solve this chaos is to concentrate on the interfaces, the exact meeting points of, for example, where your fingers touch the drumsticks, the drumsticks or hands touch the drumhead, or where the drum sound exactly activates the air molecules and then the air molecules activate the eardrums.

This is what you need to do when you are playing with anyone else – but especially in a larger group.

With such a group, for example a drum circle, it is best for just one person to begin playing and for him to interface his music with every other person in the group even though they are not playing yet. And then as each player is added, each interfaces his music similarly, until they are all playing.

And each person then integrates himself, his self as expressed through his music, with the selves being expressed by every other member of the circle.

This technique takes time and great skill, but it is essential to accomplish this, otherwise the circle can become energetic in the sense of being vigorously active, but not life energizing.

I am always reminded of this when I read such statements as "drumming is power" or "drumming for energy." But make sure that what is meant by power and energy is actually positive and life enhancing. It is so easy to fool ourselves, to actually use the power to generate energy which is more negative than positive.

Yes, drumming is power, and yes, drumming is energy. But always ask yourself, "What power? What energy?"

Time and time again, especially in groups, but also with individuals, I have heard and felt the Life Energy in their music making turn negative, debasing, rather than enhancing life. The playing may be energetic in the sense of being vigorous, but the Life Energy, the Healing Power Within is very low. And this is particularly the case with the drum, for no power can be so seductive.

"Drumming is energy" – yes, but is it Life Energy? "The power of drumming" – yes, but is it Healing Power?

The True Drummer
dedicates his music
to the enhancement
of Life Energy,
and so, too, his life.

Choose the drum
that most resonates
with your chest,
that causes it
to expand,
your heart to open.

The personalities of many musicians seem to contract when they start to play: they go into themselves rather than expanding and giving their all to the world.

Whatever his own instrument, I have him sit before the drum and play it, gently. Then to feel his chest resonating with it. And the more his chest resonates, the more his heart opens.

And now he goes back to his own instrument and tries to feel the same resonance. It will be more difficult because the drum is best for this as it is the most sympathetic of all instruments. But soon he does feel it. And he smiles.

Now his playing is generous, expansive, loving. And all thanks to the humble drum.

To find the soul
inside you,
first find it
in your drum.

The more you become
as one with the drum,
the more it seems
to play you.

What makes
one drum better
than another?
Easier for you
to find its soul.

The ring of the drum:
its soul resounding.

76

The New Rudiments

1. **Give out.** Always think of giving out: out to another, out to the world. Never try to keep the music to yourself. From the heart to the heart – that is the essence of all True Music. The drum is your heart, open in song. The music its pulse.

2. **Think up**. Aspire to the highest. As your arms and feet come down, think up – always up. Let the music lift. Let it rise up, and up.

3. **Feel the soul of your drum.** Go into it; know it. Every instrument is different – a unique soul, waiting to be invited to sing. Feel its inner essence, its Thusness. Feel it; know it – then release it into the world. To resonate with the soul of a drum, is to love it forever.

4. **Sing and play the melody**. Always sing the melody – to yourself if you must, but far better aloud. Give all of yourself, including your voice. Also, play the melody. There is rhythm in every melody and melody in every rhythm – let your drumming sing. The more you sing and play the melody, and especially the more deeply you sing, the closer you will get to the pulse of the music and thus closer to the Pulse of Life.

5. **Fred Astaire's Feet.** Concentrate on the interface of stick and skin – exactly where they meet. All creation is at the interface. Look at Astaire on the drum head. The sticks are dancing!

Give out.
Think up.
Sing the melody.
Feel the soul of the drum
– and Fred Astaire's feet.

That's all you need
to have
Spirit in your drumming.

$\mathcal{W}$hy does the drum, of all instruments, have the greatest potential for life enhancement? I don't really know but here are some thoughts.

First of all there are no notes, therefore fewer judgements to be made by yourself and by others. There will be less right and wrong – especially if there is no counting.

Is it the vibrating membrane? So alive!

Is it because of its roundness?

What I do know, is that everyone's association with the drum is with Life, with Heart – and even more with the Mother.

My heart is like
my drum.
If I tune it,
just so,
and play
on the Pulse,
all the other drums
resonate with it.

They are not called
musical instruments
just because
they make it:
they themselves
are music,
our fingers
transporting their song
into the audible world.

We are blessed
having so many colors
on our palette:
all the drums,
and cymbals, and traps,
So many colors!

All other instruments
are monochrome.
We're a rainbow!

The drum set is the most adaptable
of all instruments.
Every piece can be arranged
and positioned, tuned, and integrated,
optimized,
for the transmission of the highest Life Energy,
the greatest Healing Power.

Think how lucky you are!
The other players have just a chair,
you have an adjustable stool.
So too does the pianist
– but he can't also raise the piano
to just the right height for him.

Drummers are
the most
enlightened:
their trap-table
toys,
for them,
make music.

I love all my drums
for every one
makes my chest
resonate with it.

Rattles, bells
and whistles –
our exciting,
wonderful toys!
We can be
as happy as kids

I own many drums. And I love them all, for I feel into them all. I play one, going deep into it, becoming one with its soul, then allowing it to play me. And then with another. And from their souls to the souls of the other musicians, and the audience.

A different drum, a different soul, for a different song, for a different me.

If violins were as inexpensive as drums, the violinist might become as empathetic, as all-feeling, as the drummer.

———————

If I really loved my drums,
I'd be glad
to give them away.

If I really
loved life,
I'd have no fear
of death.

                    If I really believed
                    there was life
                    after death,
                    I'd be buried
                    with my drums.

Some True Drumming Basics

♦ Every musician emphasizes a different aspect of the totality of the song. Yours is the most important – for rhythm is the most basic as it commences at the beginning of life, in the womb.

♦ Choose the drum whose soul you can most easily find. This will be the one that most expands your chest, opens your heart.

♦ Feel your chest resonate with the drum.

♦ The more the palms are up, the more you can give.

♦ As your arms come down, think up – always up. Let the music lift. Let it rise up.

♦ Loose wrists, body free. Let your whole body do the playing.

♦ Love your left hand. It wants to play easier – and it will.

♦ Concentrate on the interface of stick and head. Exactly where they meet, every time they do. All creation is at the interface.

- Look at the stick heads dancing like Fred Astaire's feet.

- Be free – take risks. You are safe.

- Always play the melody – and sing it.

- Hear the lullaby in the bass. Feel it. Let it roll around and around.

- Imagine the drum is your heart, open in song. The music its pulse.

- Be always aware of your breath. Never jam it. It must always be free, for only then are you free. You can't breathe freely to a metronome or click track. For they are the beat. The free breath ebbs and flows to its own deep pulsations.

- The drum kit is the greatest musical invention. For, albeit by accident, it comes closest to our ideal of musical instruments being designed for their highest therapeutic power.

- We have yet to have musical instruments specifically designed to be healing, to transmit Therapeutic Power. By fortuitous accident, drums, especially the snare, most approach this ideal.

- The drum set is the most adjustable of all instruments. Every piece can be arranged and positioned, tuned, and integrated, optimized for the transmission of the highest Life Energy, the greatest Healing.

- Think how lucky you are! The other players have just a chair, you have an adjustable stool. So too does the pianist – but he can't also raise the piano to just the right height for him.

- When you are playing on the Pulse, it feels like the drum is playing you.

- Get on the wave of the Pulse, and ride it effortlessly all the way to the beach.

- I am real, I'm alive, I breathe. I pulsate. I am not a machine. If they want the beat, they can buy a metronome.

- Don't count – feel. When the math comes in, the joy goes out.

- Play with joy, with a smile. If you aren't enjoying it – stop.

- Never practice – that's just the brain. Always play, even if the audience is afar. That's the heart as well.

- Don't judge your playing – for then it is not play, but hard work. Just aim to refine your intention.

- It's so easy to be seduced into playing the drums for sex. But that's not love.

- Think of the drum as your mother. Are you treating her right?

- Remember it's an instrument of love – not war.

- It's not the volume, but the intensity of the feeling, at even the quietest level.

- Feel the Music flowing through all of your body.

- Come forward into the music, into the audience, into yourself.

- Don't play the drums – allow them to play you. This is called the transcendental experience.

- Always keep in mind that all of you, your Totality – body, mind, and spirit – is transmitted in each and every note.

- Give all of yourself. This is me. Here I am. All of me, now.

- Play with all your heart: wholehearted. And with Passion: all your fire, filled with Enthusiasm.

Music can be the easiest way to Heaven on earth – if we want it to be.

—————

The True Drummer
aspires
to assist Music
to fulfil Its promise
as the ultimate
Healing Power.

First,
the drums legato,
then, at last,
your life.

Music
is our Salvation.

Play your drum –
proclaim
Its coming.

What am I really trying to say?

There is a Way – the way the universe, this world, this person, and all around him, goes.

This Way is outside me, and also inside – as my deepest self, my Muse.

The more I accept this Way, inner and outer, (they are one) – the less will I suffer in life.

And it's my way to be offered ways to better know and accept the Way – and my way is the degree that I do accept and allow It.

And it is my way to learn that the easiest way to first find the Way is through a song – the way it goes, really goes.

And the easiest way to do this is to sing and dance and drum on the Pulse, for It is the Way of Music – and of Life.

———

One day, well in the future,
Music will at last become
the Great Therapy.
And the drums of this present age
will then be acknowledged
as the first instruments
that helped Music
to ultimately fulfill
Its long-anticipated promise.

When I was a little fellow in New Orleans, I wanted to be a doctor ...

But I enjoyed every minute of my life drumming. My enjoyment, that I was getting out of music, I was sending through to others. I know that some of my drumming touched a lot of people's hearts. If someone was angry, even with domestic troubles, hanging where I was drumming – drumming with my heart – they'd just forget their troubles and be happy. Even if I'd been a doctor, I couldn't have done any more than that.

BABY DODDS

Yes, Baby, I also came to believe that music can heal, ultimately more than medicine, for It can heal the soul. I, too, play to heal.

But I also encourage all sufferers to themselves drum, for what they give is so much more important than what they receive.

And so often I play your recordings to them as an inspiration. For you said it all: "Drumming is Spirit."

One day Music will be recognized as the greatest Healing Power. Our task is to help It fulfill its promise, to bring that day a little closer.

———————

John Diamond, M.D.

Dr. John Diamond graduated from Sydney University Medical School in 1957 and obtained his Diploma in Psychological Medicine in 1962. He is a Fellow of the Royal Australian and New Zealand College of Psychiatry, a Foundation Member of the Royal College of Psychiatrists and past President of the International Academy of Preventive Medicine.

Dr. Diamond, as the Founder of The Institute for Music and Health, has investigated, researched and applied many factors in the musician and his instruments in an attempt to maximize music's therapeutic power. A healer, author, photographer, poet, composer and musician, playing drums, percussion and the didjeridu, he has taught countless musicians and artists, and his knowledge extends to all genres of music, especially classical and jazz.

As a Holistic Consultant, Dr. Diamond continues to devote his life and work to helping people gratefully embrace all of life and its vicissitudes. His concept of the Pulse is the culmination of forty years in medicine, psychiatry, complementary medicine, the humanities, holistic healing and the arts.

———